THE PORTABLE CRAFTER™
QUILTING

THE PORTABLE CRAFTER™
QUILTING

Mary Jo Hiney

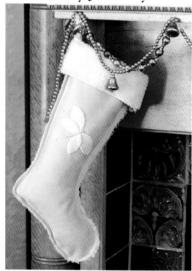

Sterling Publishing Co., Inc.
New York
A Sterling/Chapelle Book

If you have questions or comments, please contact:
Chapelle, Ltd., Inc.,
P.O. Box 9252, Ogden, UT 84409
(801) 621-2777 • (801) 621-2788 Fax
e-mail: chapelle@chapelleltd.com
web site: chapelleltd.com

Library of Congress
Cataloging-in-Publication Data on request

Credits
Jo Packham
Sara Toliver
Cindy Stoeckl

10 9 8 7 6 5 4 3 2 1

Editor/book design: Laura Best

Copy editor: Marilyn Goff

Photography: Ryne Hazen, Zac Williams

Published by Sterling Publishing Co., Inc.
387 Park Avenue South, New York, NY 10016
©2005 by Mary Jo Hiney
Distributed in Canada by Sterling Publishing
c/o Canadian Manda Group, 165 Dufferin Street
Toronto, Ontario, Canada M6K 3H6
Distributed in Great Britain by Chrysalis Books Group PLC
The Chrysalis Building, Bramley Road, London W10 6SP, England
Distributed in Australia by Capricorn Link (Australia) Pty. Ltd.
P.O. Box 704, Windsor, NSW 2756, Australia
Printed in China
All Rights Reserved

Sterling ISBN 1-4027-1874-8

For information about custom editions, special sales, premium and corporate purchases, please contact Sterling Special Sales Department at 800-805-5489 or specialsales@sterlingpub.com

TABLE OF CONTENTS

Introduction 6
Quilting Basics 7
Yo-yo Eyeglass Case 14
Elephant Appliqué
    Cosmetic Case 18
Robbing Peter to Pay
    Paul Coin Purse 23
Designer Shoe
    Travel Pouch 28
Dutch Windmill
    Stocking 33
Crazy-quilted Wallet 38
Silk Appliqué Handbag . . 44
Loved Hangings 50

Mohawk Trail Handbag . . 54
Wool Appliqué Pillow . . . 60
Clamshell Appliqué
    Pillow 63
Sailboat Appliqué Pillow . 69
Dresden Plate with
    Hexagons Pillow 74
Violet Stencil Pillow 78
Oversized Rose Canvas . . 82
Children Wall Hanging . . 86
Butterfly Christmas
    Stocking 92
Metric Conversion Chart . 95
Index 96

INTRODUCTION

Quilting is one of those creative enterprises that can be accomplished on a small scale or a large scale, and in which all elements can be sewn by hand. The projects throughout this book have been created to be easily transported and so that they have an enjoyable amount of hand-stitching along with advance preparation time. It is entirely up to you as to the amount of hand- or machine-sewing each project will entail. You will pleasantly discover that hand-appliqué and other hand-quilting work is a very simple process that does not require a great deal of time.

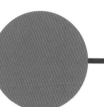

QUILTING BASICS

GENERAL NOTIONS & TOOLS

Cotton swab
Fray preventative
Grid-lined ruler
Hand-stitching needles
Iron/ironing board
Pencil
Photocopier
Posterboard
Quilter's freezer paper (appliqué)
Quilter's ruler
Quilting pins
Rotary cutter
Safety pins
Scissors: craft, fabric
Seam ripper
Self-healing cutting mat
Sewing machine
Sewing-machine needles
Spray starch
Straight pins
Tape measure

Threads: matching, neutral
Tracing paper
Water-filled spray/mist bottle
Water-soluble fabric-marking pen
Zipper-foot attachment for sewing
    machine

*Keeping projects and supplies together
in a small travel bag, makes projects
easier to take on the go.*

APPLYING A ZIPPER

Use a zipper that is longer than the project's opening. The zipper may be trimmed once it has been secured. Pin pressed or folded edge of fabric to left edge of zipper tape, aligning pressed fabric edge to edge of zipper coil. Begin and end zipper where designated in instructions.

Using a zipper foot, machine-sew pressed edge to zipper tape. Align and  sew opposite pressed edge of fabric to opposite side of zipper tape. *Note: The zipper may be hand-stitched if desired.*

BASTING

It may be helpful to position design elements on the background fabric prior to sewing them in place. To eliminate pin frustration, baste-stitch elements in place. While appliquéing, additional pins can be used on the piece being stitched.

BATTING

Batting is used as the middle layer of a quilted project. There are numerous types of batting available. Bonded cotton batting gives a flat, natural appearance. Fusible fleece is useful for small projects.

BEADING

Several needle types can be used for beading. The obvious choice is the beading needle. For some beads, it is the only needle that will slide through a bead hole. Other needle choices include a fine embroidery needle and a milliner's needle.

Use doubled thread to stitch beads in place. Bring needle to the surface at desired location. Slip needle through bead or beads and position them at thread entry point. Stitch thread through fabric at opposite end of bead or beads and back to original entry point. Stitch through beads again, double-stitching them in place. Working with same thread length, continue to stitch beads.

BINDING

To bind a quilt, cut a straight piece of fabric the length of the edge to be finished plus 1½". The width can vary according to the desired binding size. For ¼" finished binding, cut strips 1⅜" wide. For ½" binding, cut strips 2⅜" wide. If necessary, piece lengths together by diagonally cutting ends to be pieced, then sewing ends, using ¼" seam allowance. Press length in half, matching long edges. Align long raw edges with quilt edge and sew layers together. Press binding outward, then fold it around to the back side. Position folded edge of binding over binding seam line and hand- or machine-stitch binding in place. When necessary, fold ends under before folding binding around to the back side.

EDGE-PRESSING

Edge-pressing is a preliminary pressing step that exposes the seam line when turned right side out. It is used when it is not possible to press a seam allowance open. Unlike pressing a seam allowance open, only one side of the seam allowance is pressed. To do this, fold over the top layer of a seam allowance and press.

PRESSING

Pressing is a key factor with any project. For ease of travel, an appliqué iron and small padded surface can be used to prepare appliqué pieces for any of the projects. Have handy a water-filled spray/mist bottle. Always test a scrap of fabric for heat resistance prior to pressing. If too hot, an iron can melt and/or scorch fibers. A presscloth is a handy helper as well when pressing.

EMBROIDERY STITCHES
Backstitch
1. Bring needle up at A; go down at B. Up at C; down at A. Up at D; down at C. Continue.

Bullion
1. Bring needle up at A and down at B.

2. Bring needle back up at A. Do not pull needle through. Wind floss around needle a number of times.

3. Hold coil and needle firmly with thumb and forefinger and pull needle and ribbon through coil.

4. Turn coil back and insert needle back into fabric at B. To make bullion curve more, wind more floss.

Bullion Lazy Daisy
1. Bring needle up at A. Go down at B and up at C, but do not pull through.

2. Snugly wrap floss around needle tip one to three times. Holding finger over wrapped floss, pull needle through floss and down through fabric.

Couching
1. Come up at A and down at B to create a straight stitch base. Come up at C and down at D. Continue across straight stitch base.

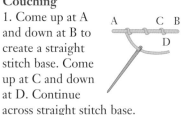

French Knot
1. Bring needle up at A. Wrap floss around needle once. Holding floss securely off to one side, go down at B near A. Do not allow knot to pass through material.

Lazy Daisy

1. Bring needle up at A. Go down at B as close to A as possible, but not into A. Bring needle tip up at C and form loop around needle.

2. Go down at D. Pull needle through.

Whipstitch

1. Bring needle through fabric at A. Cross over fabric opening. Bring thread through other side at B. Repeat until desired length is stitched together. Be certain to keep stitches uniform in length and distance.

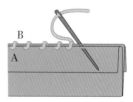

FREEZER PAPER TECHNIQUE

Note: If necessary, make certain to enlarge pattern to required percentage on photocopier.

1. Trace or photocopy appliqué pattern onto paper. Cut out paper pattern.

2. Reverse and tape or trace appliqué pattern onto matte side of freezer paper. Cut out.

3. Press shiny side of freezer-paper face downward onto wrong side of appliqué fabric.

4. Cut fabric appliqué, leaving a ¼" seam allowance around freezer paper pattern, or as indicated in instructions. Spray a bit of spray starch into a small container. Saturate cotton swab with spray starch. Dab outer edge of fabric with swab. Clip outer edge of fabric up to freezer paper.

5. Using iron, steam-press outer edges of fabric up over edge of freezer paper, being careful to maintain appliqué shape.

5

6. Remove freezer paper and press again.

6

7. Using single or doubled thread, hand-appliqué the outer edge of appliqué in place.

7

MAKING YO-YOS

1. Using needle and doubled thread, knot ends together.

2. With fabric circle wrong side up, fold a scant ⅛" edge of circle to wrong side while gather-stitching along folded edge.

3. Pull on thread allowing gathered edges to cup toward the center. Secure gathers by knotting thread. When making more than one yo-yo keep the tension consistent so yo-yos look consistent.

NEEDLE-TURN TECHNIQUE

Some fabrics and shapes are less cooperative than desired when using the freezer paper technique. When this occurs, use the needle-turn technique when appliquéing.

1. Using a pencil, outline pattern shape onto right side of fabric.

2. Pin appliqué piece in place.

3. With single-strand thread, use needle to roll raw edge of fabric under up to traced line for approximately 1" in length, clipping inward curves and points as necessary up to traced line. Appliqué that space in place.

4. Continue to work appliqué piece in this manner.

TRANSFERRING AN APPLIQUÉ DESIGN ONTO FABRIC

Some designs will need to be marginally transferred onto the background fabric, such as a starting position or general outline. Usually, it is not necessary to transfer the entire design. Tape design to a light source, such as a window or a lightbox. Center and tape fabric over design. Using a pencil, trace over key elements of the design.

You will find the appliqué patterns and prepared pieces to be the most accurate way to create an appliquéd design.

WORKING WITH PATTERNS

Photocopy the patterns required, enlarging them if necessary.

For some patterns, it will be helpful to make a template from posterboard. Tracing around small patterns made from posterboard is easier than working with a paper pattern. Make certain that patterns remain accurate when re-created.

Yo-yo
Eyeglass Case

NEEDED ITEMS
- Silk dupioni fabrics
    - (6½" x 10" each) for yo-yos
        - Bright blue
        - Bright plum
        - Fuchsia
        - Lime green
        - Orange
        - Rich gold
    - (7½" x 8" each) for eyeglass case
        - Cobalt
        - Seafoam
- Fusible fleece (6½" x 7")
- Fusible interfacing (2 pieces 7½" x 8")
- General Notions & Tools on page 7

SIZE
7" x 3¼"

INSTRUCTIONS

PREPARATION

1. Using Yo-yo Pattern on page 17, cut six circles from each of the following silk fabrics: bright blue, bright plum, fuchsia, lime green, orange, and rich gold.

YO-YOS

1. *Refer to Making Yo-yos on page 12.* Hand-stitch each circle into a yo-yo.

2. Refer to Yo-yo Assembly Diagram to stitch yo-yos together in rows. With gathered-center sides facing, stitch two rich gold yo-yos together, taking three small

stitches along the center edge. Continue to stitch rich gold yo-yos together in this manner, forming a column. Repeat for each color.

3. With gathered center sides facing, stitch rich gold column to bright plum column, taking three small stitches along center edge of each yo-yo. Continue to stitch columns together.

4. Join last yo-yo to first yo-yo along each row, forming a tube shape with horizontal stripes. Turn right side out.

EYEGLASS CASE
1. Fuse interfacing onto wrong sides of cobalt and seafoam silk pieces.

2. Fuse fleece onto wrong side of cobalt piece.

3. Using a ½" seam allowance, hand- or machine-sew cobalt and seafoam pieces together, right sides facing, along 7½" edges. Press seam allowance open.

4. Fold and pin piece in half, right sides facing, aligning long edges, matching the seam line intersection.

YO-YO ASSEMBLY DIAGRAM

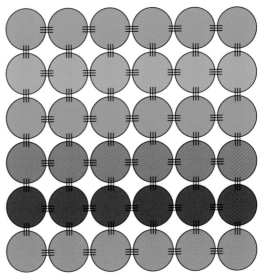

5. Sew long edges together forming a tube. Press seam allowance toward cobalt piece. Turn right side out.

6. Fold cobalt side along seam line toward inside of tube.

7. Position seam line centered on one side of the tube. Sew short raw edges together. Trim seam allowance to ¼". Overcast. Turn tube cobalt side out.

FINISH
1. Slip yo-yo tube over eyeglass case. Hand-stitch yo-yos to case along top and bottom edges.

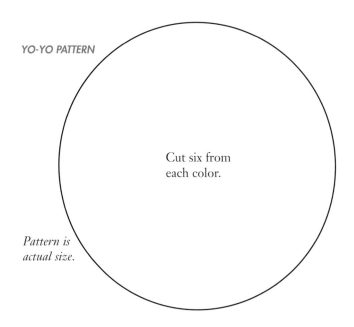

YO-YO PATTERN

Cut six from
each color.

*Pattern is
actual size.*

ELEPHANT APPLIQUÉ
COSMETIC CASE

NEEDED ITEMS

- Cotton fabrics
  - Black/pink stripes (2¼" x width of goods) for gussets
  - Black/polka dots (6" x 18") for back and front
  - Fuchsia print (2½" sq.) for elephant appliqué
  - Pink print (7" x 3") for ear, elephant
- Black beads
  - Bugles (3)
  - Rhinestones, 3mm (7)
  - Rice-shaped, 2mm x 4mm (11)
  - Seeds, 11/0 (26)
  - Teardrop-shaped, 6mm (2)
- Embroidery floss, fuchsia (scrap)
- Iron-on vinyl (¼ yd. optional)
- Satin ribbon, ¼"-wide fuchsia (9")
- Spray adhesive
- Zipper, black (7"–9")
- General Notions & Tools on page 7

SIZE
6½" x 4" x 1½"

INSTRUCTIONS

Note: Seam allowance ⅜" unless otherwise indicated.

PREPARATION

1. Using Elephant Purse Pattern on page 21, cut one front and back from polka-dotted fabric. From striped fabric, cut one lower gusset 13⅛" x 2¼". Cut two zipper strips 7¾" x 2". *Optional: From iron-on vinyl, cut two fronts and one lower gusset.*

1. Using Elephant Appliqué A and B on page 21, trace one each backward onto dull side of freezer paper. Cut out.

2. *Refer to Freezer Paper Technique on pages 11–12.* Iron A onto wrong side of pink print fabric. Iron B onto wrong side of fuchsia print fabric.

3. Trim A seam allowance to ¼". Dab seam allowance with spray starch. Clip seam allowance to paper edge.

4. Press fabric edges over edge of freezer paper. Remove freezer paper and press again. Trim fabric sides of B seam allowance to ¼". Press fabric edge over edge of freezer paper, but do not press upper edge over.

5. Position B onto elephant. Hand-stitch sides in place. Wrap top edge of B over top of elephant.

6. Layer two scraps from pink print fabric, with right sides facing. Trace C backward onto wrong side of pink print fabric. Sew side and bottom edges on traced line. Trim seam allowance to ⅛". Turn right side out through top edge. Press.

7. Turn raw edge of C under ¼". Appliqué onto elephant along top edge, leaving remainder of C unstitched.

8. *Optional: Fuse iron-on vinyl onto wrong side of front. Repeat for back.*

9. Bead side edges of B with seed and rice-shaped beads, having one teardrop bead at center bottom of appliqué. Bead upper edge on face with bugle and seed beads. Bead lower edge on face with seed beads alternated with glued-on rhinestones. Stitch teardrop-shaped bead to face for eye.

ELEPHANT APPLIQUÉ PATTERNS

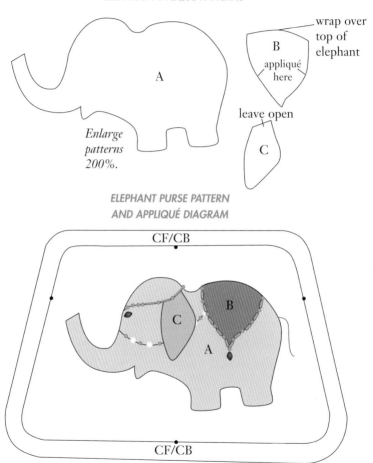

A

B
appliqué here

wrap over top of elephant

leave open

C

Enlarge patterns 200%.

ELEPHANT PURSE PATTERN AND APPLIQUÉ DIAGRAM

CF/CB

B

C

A

CF/CB

Enlarge pattern 200%.

1. Press zipper strips in half, matching long edges.

2. *Refer to Applying a Zipper on page 8.* Stitch pressed edge of zipper strips to zipper tape.

3. *Optional: Fuse iron-on vinyl to wrong side of lower gusset.* Sew short ends of lower gusset to ends of zipper strips, right sides facing. Press seam allowances open.

4. Stay-stitch gusset/zipper strip long edges along seam line. Clip gusset/zipper strip to stay-stitching.

5. Fold gusset/zipper strip in half, aligning short seams. Mark fold along both edges. *Note: The mark between zipper strips is top center front and back. The mark between lower gusset is bottom center front and back.*

6. Sew one long edge of gusset/zipper strip to outer edge of front, matching top and bottom center fronts. Trim seam allowance to ⅛". Overcast. Repeat for back.

FINISH
1. Slip ribbon through zipper pull. Tie ends together. Coat ends with fray preventative. When dry, trim at a slant.

2. Using floss, stitch elephant's tail in place.

ROBBING PETER TO PAY PAUL
COIN PURSE

NEEDED ITEMS

- Cotton fabrics
    Apricot print (3" x 16") for patchwork
    Fuchsia print (3" x 16") for patchwork
    Fuchsia print (7" x 15") for zipper strips, bottom, lining
    Orange print (3" x 16") for patchwork
    Pink batik (3" x 16") for patchwork
- Fusible fleece (7" x 10")
- Zipper, pink (7"–9")
- General Notions & Tools on page 7

SIZE
4" x 6" x 1"

INSTRUCTIONS
PREPARATION

1. Cut six 2½" squares from each of the four patchwork fabrics.

2. Using Robbing Peter to Pay Paul Appliqué Pattern B on page 26, cut two from freezer paper.

3. *Refer to Freezer Paper Technique on pages 11–12.* Iron one freezer-paper piece onto wrong side of one pink batik square. Trim seam allowance from curved sides to ¼".

4. Dab curved-edge seam allowance with spray starch. Clip seam allowance to curved paper edge. Press curved fabric edges over edge of freezer paper. Remove freezer paper and press again.

5. Repeat Steps 3–4 for each pink batik and apricot print squares.

6. Pin pink pieces onto orange print squares. Pin apricot pieces onto fuchsia print square.

APPLIQUÉ

1. Hand-stitch curved edges of each appliqué piece onto each backdrop square.

PATCHWORK

Note: Hand- or machine-sew using ¼" seam allowances.

1. Press appliquéd squares.

2. *Refer to Robbing Peter to Pay Paul Assembly Diagram on page 27.* Sew two orange and one fuchsia squares together, alternating shades, matching all intersections. Press seam allowances open.

3. Sew two fuchsia and one orange squares together, alternating shades, matching all intersections. Press seam allowances open.

4. Sew the two sets together, matching all intersections, forming coin purse front. Press seam allowances open.

5. Repeat Steps 2–4 for remaining appliquéd squares, forming coin purse back.

COIN PURSE ASSEMBLY

1. Using A for lining, cut one along fold, cut two zipper strips 1" x 6½", and cut one bottom strip 1½" x 5½" from fuchsia print.

2. Using A for lining, cut one along fold from fusible fleece. Trim seam allowance on all edges to ¼".

3. Sew one long edge of bottom strip centered to bottom edge of front, right sides facing. *Note: front is wider than bottom strip.* Sew remaining long edge of bottom strip centered to bottom edge of back, right sides facing. Press seam allowances toward bottom strip.

4. Fuse fleece to wrong side of assembled piece.

ZIPPER

1. *Refer to Applying a Zipper on page 8.* Sew one long edge of a zipper

Small Bugle Beads
For Needlework Projects

strip to top edge of front, right sides facing. Press seam allowance toward strip. Sew one long edge of remaining zipper strip to top edge of back in the same manner.

2. Press and wrap zipper strips over seam allowance and around to wrong side of assembled piece. Pin in place.

3. Sew pressed edges of zipper strips to zipper tape. Sew again a scant ¼" from first row of stitching.

FINISHING

1. Pin and sew front and back together, right sides facing, along the side edges. Press seam allowances open.

2. To make corners, fold end from side seams to meet center of bottom strip, with right sides facing. Sew across corners. Press open.

3. Sew lining front and back together, right sides facing, along the side edges. Press seam

allowances open. Stitch corners as with Step 2. Press upper edge of lining under ⅜" to wrong side.

4. Slip lining into coin purse. Hand-stitch upper edge of lining to inside of coin purse along zipper tape.

ROBBING PETER TO PAY PAUL
APPLIQUÉ PATTERNS

A

Place on fold.

Enlarge patterns 170%.

B

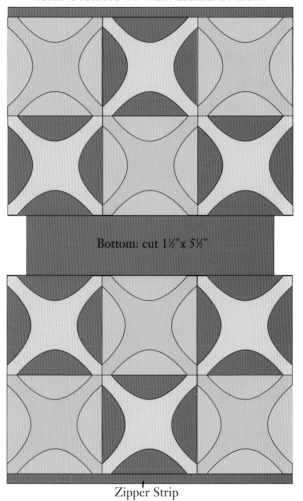

Bottom: cut 1½"x 5½"

Zipper Strip

DESIGNER SHOE
TRAVEL POUCH

NEEDED ITEMS

- Cotton fabrics
    Prints
        Black/ecru (2" x 8") for C
        Black/ecru polka dots (6" x 7") for shoe appliqué
        Black/ecru striped (½ yd) for E, F, lining
        Ecru/black (12½" x 14") for D
    Solids
        Dark oatmeal (4½" x 8") for B
        Oatmeal (8" sq.) for A
- Embroidery floss, black
- Ribbons
    Black/ecru stripes, 1½"-wide (2¼ yd)
    Ecru/black stripes, ⅜"-wide (¾ yd)
- General Notions & Tools on page 7

SIZE
14½" x 10"

INSTRUCTIONS
Note: Seam allowances ½" unless otherwise indicated.

PREPARATION
1. From striped fabric, cut one strip 2½" x 21" for E, one piece 5" x 21" for F, and one piece 14" x 21" for lining.

APPLIQUÉ
1. Using Shoe Appliqué Pattern on page 30, trace shoe backward onto dull side of freezer paper. Cut out.

2. *Refer to Freezer Paper Technique on pages 11–12.* Iron shoe appliqué

28

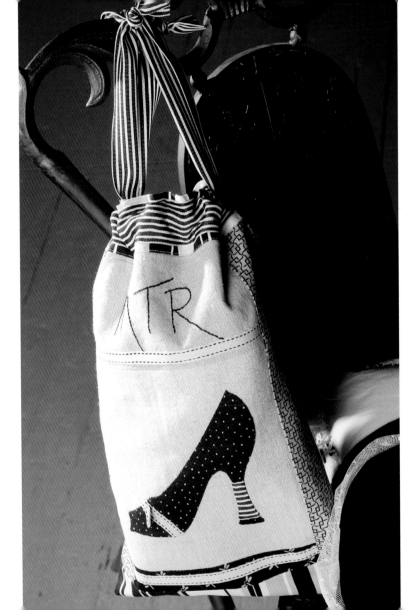

onto wrong side of black with polka-dot fabric. Trim seam allowance to ¼".

3. Dab seam allowance with spray starch. Clip seam allowance to paper edge at curves. Press fabric edges over edge of freezer paper. Remove freezer paper and press again.

4. Wrap a piece of 1½"-wide ribbon around heel. Hand-stitch in place.

5. Wrap a piece of ⅜"-wide ribbon across front of shoe, forming a small half bow. Hand-stitch in place.

6. Center and pin shoe onto right side of oatmeal square A. Appliqué in place.

MONOGRAM

1. Choose a font style or create original lettering. Using a pencil, center and draw 1½"-tall initials of choice onto dark oatmeal B.

2. Backstitch initials with three strands of black floss. Press.

TRAVEL POUCH ASSEMBLY

1. *Refer to Travel Pouch Assembly Diagram on page 31.* To form travel pouch center piece, hand- or machine-sew top edge of A to bottom edge of B. Sew the bottom edge of A to one edge of C. Press seam allowances open.

2. Hand-stitch ⅛"-wide ribbon to bottom edge of B, ¼" up from seam line. Hand-stitch ⅛"-wide ribbon to top edge of C, ¼" down from seam line.

3. Sew long edges of D to left and right edges of center piece, forming a tube. Press seam allowances toward D.

SHOE APPLIQUÉ PATTERN

Ribbon

Enlarge pattern 200%.

Striped Ribbon

4. Sew short ends of E together, right sides facing. Press seam allowance open. Sew to bottom edge of tube, placing E seam line at center back of tube. Press seam allowance toward E.

5. Turn inside out. Position with center piece centered between back and side edges of D.

LINING

1. Sew 14" lining edges together, right sides facing. Press seam open. Turn right side out.

2. Slip lining over tube, wrong sides facing. Position seam line at center back and flatten tube with center piece centered as in Step 3 for Travel Pouch Assembly.

TRAVEL POUCH ASSEMBLY DIAGRAM

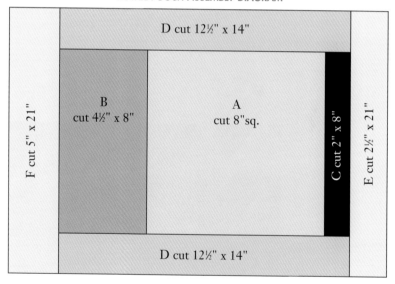

F cut 5" x 21"

D cut 12½" x 14"

B
cut 4½" x 8"

A
cut 8"sq.

C cut 2" x 8"

E cut 2½" x 21"

D cut 12½" x 14"

3. Sew tube and lining together along bottom edge. Trim seam allowance to ¼". Overcast. Turn right side out. Press bottom edge.

FINISHING

1. Sew short ends of F together, right sides facing. Press seam allowance open.

2. Sew one long edge of F to top edge of line at center back. Press seam allowance toward F.

3. Cut two 11" lengths from 1½"-wide ribbon. Fold ends under ½".

4. To form casing, sew top and bottom ribbon edges to F, placing bottom ribbon edge ¼" up from seam line and having turned-under edges meet at the pouch sides. Do not sew across turned-under edges.

5. Fold upper edge of F under ½". Fold

F down to meet lined pouch/F seam line. Sew folded-under edge in place, enclosing seam line.

6. For handles, cut remaining 1½"-wide ribbon into two lengths. Slip one length through and around casing's right-side opening. Slip remaining length through and around casing's left-side opening.

7. Tie ends from one handle together in a knot. Coat ends with fray preventative. Let dry. Repeat for other handle.

8. Trim ribbon ends. Pull on both ribbons to close pouch.

DUTCH WINDMILL
STOCKING

NEEDED ITEMS
- Cotton fabrics
  - Ecru broadcloth (½ yd) for piecework, stocking lining
  - Red broadcloth (½ yd) for binding band, piecework, stocking back
- Cotton batting, 44"-wide (¼ yd)
- General Notions & Tools on page 7

SIZE
8" x 18"

INSTRUCTIONS
PREPARATION
1. *Refer to Dutch Windmill Patterns on page 37.* Using A, cut 15 each from red and ecru broadcloths.

2. Using B, cut 32 each from red and ecru broadcloths.

3. Cut one stocking from red broadcloth and cut two from ecru broadcloth. Cut two from batting.

4. Cut top binding strip 16" x 3" from red broadcloth. Cut batting strip 16" x 2½".

5. Cut loop piece 6" x 1¼" from red broadcloth.

APPLIQUÉ
Note: Using pieces cut from B, prepare 27 of each shade for appliqué. Do not prepare remaining five pieces indicated with an "x" on the Dutch Windmill Stocking Piecework Diagram on page 37, as it is not necessary for these pieces to be appliquéd.

1. Using C, cut one from posterboard, or cut six from quilter's freezer paper. *Notes: If using posterboard, prepare each piece as follows: Place posterboard template onto a Pattern B fabric piece (wrong side up, if you have chosen to work with prints rather than solids.) Dab curved-edge seam allowance with spray starch. Press curved fabric edge up over edge of template. Remove template and press again. Reuse template. For each piece, prepare the curved edge only for appliqué.*

If using freezer paper, press shiny side of paper template onto wrong side of fabric piece. Dab curved-edge seam allowance with spray starch. Press curved fabric edge over edge of template. Remove template and press again. Reuse template. For each piece, prepare the curved edge only for appliqué.

2. Pin B pieces onto A triangles where indicated on pattern by dotted lines. Pin ecru pieces to top and bottom corners of twelve red A triangles. Pin remaining ecru pieces to either the top or bottom corner as indicated on piecework

diagram. Pin red pieces to top and bottom corners of twelve ecru A triangles as well, pinning the remaining red pieces to either the top or bottom corner as indicated on piecework diagram. Appliqué pieces in place. Press.

STOCKING FRONT
1. Use ¼" seam allowances for piecework. Press seam allowances open for piecework. Sew pieces together in horizontal rows.

2. Begin by sewing ecru and red appliquéd A triangles together along diagonal edge. For those spaces marked with an "x," sew straight edge of B piece to diagonal edge of appliquéd A triangle piece (or to straight edge of another B piece).

3. Sew pieces together to form horizontal rows.

STOCKING
1. Cut stocking shape from pieced front.

2. Layer and pin together lining, batting, and front stocking pieces. Repeat for back stocking, batting, and lining and pieces.

3. Place layered pieces with front and back sides facing. Using ¼" seam allowance, sew along side and bottom edges. Overcast seam allowance. Clip curves to seam line. Press seam allowances toward back as much as possible.

4. Press long edges of loop piece under ¼". Press piece in half, aligning pressed-under edges.

5. Whipstitch edges together.

6. Fold loop in half, matching ends. Pin ends to stocking's left-side seam allowance along top edge.

7. Layer top binding and top batting pieces, aligning short ends and one long edge. Using ¼" seam allowance, sew short

ends together. Press seam allowance open.

8. Sew binding edge (with batting) around top edge of stocking, right sides facing, matching binding seam with left-side stocking seam. Press seam allowance toward binding.

BINDING AND FINISHING
1. Fold binding in half and over to inside, and fold remaining binding edge under ½". Hand-stitch edge in place.

2. Fold loop up onto binding from inside and hand-stitch to binding.

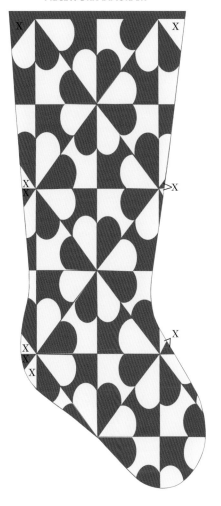

**DUTCH WINDMILL
PIECEWORK DIAGRAM**

X   X

X
X   X

X
X X

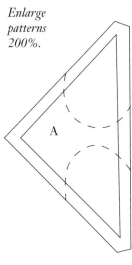

**DUTCH WINDMILL
PATTERNS**

C

*Enlarge
patterns
200%.*

A

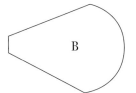

B

37

CRAZY-QUILTED
WALLET

NEEDED ITEMS

- Fabrics
    Muslin (4" x 8") for crazy-quilt front foundation
    Silks (totaling 7½" x 9")
        Celedon green, for Outer Binding E, spaces 3, 11
        Dusty orchid, for Bottom Pockets D, space 8
        Dusty plum, for inside Overall Piece A, spaces 5, 14
        Mauve, for Full Pocket B, spaces 4, 12
        Pale blush, for Full Pocket B lining, spaces 6, 10
        Salmon (3" sq.) for spaces 2, 13
        Terra-cotta, for Slant Pockets C, space 9
- Color image or photograph of choice, printed on printer
    fabric or canvas sheet (2)
- Embroidery floss, assorted shades
- Fusible interfacing (½ yd)
- General Notions & Tools on page 7

SIZE
7" x 3½"

INSTRUCTIONS
PREPARATION
1. Using Crazy-quilted Wallet Pattern on page 42, cut one A from dusty plum. Cut one interfacing piece.

2. Cut two B from mauve. Cut two interfacing pieces.

3. Cut two B lining from pale blush. Cut two interfacing pieces.

4. Cut four (two left- and two right-facing) C from terra-cotta. Cut two (one left- and one right-facing) interfacing pieces.

5. Cut four D from dusty orchid. Cut two interfacing pieces.

6. Cut one E 4½" x 7½" from celadon. Cut one interfacing piece.

1. Trim image or photo to 2⅜" square. If desired, use Crazy-quilted Wallet Diagram 1 below as your image, color-copied onto printer fabric or canvas sheet. An enlargement of the image can be used in the crazy quilting. Another option would be to draw and color-in your own artwork, either on fabric or paper. If on paper, color-copy the art onto printed fabric or canvas sheet.

2. *Refer to Crazy-quilted Wallet Diagram 1.* Position image on muslin. Hand-stitch in place along edges.

3. *Refer to Crazy-quilted Wallet Diagram 2 on page 43.* Appliqué silk scraps around image, working fabrics in numerical order. Include scraps from image or photo in spaces 7 and 15. If desired, create your own random crazy-quilted pattern.

4. Using floss, embroider crazy-quilted wallet front as desired.

Note: Use ½" seam allowance unless otherwise indicated.
1. Fuse interfacing onto wrong sides of silk fabric pieces A–E.

2. Trim crazy-quilt wallet front to 3½" x 7½".

3. Sew Outer Binding E (4½" x

CRAZY-QUILTED WALLET DIAGRAM 1

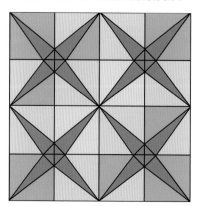

3. Sew Outer Binding E (4½" x 7½") to left-side edge of front, right sides facing. Press seam allowance toward outer binding.

4. Refer to C Sewing Diagram. Sew two C pieces (one left- and two right-facing) together, right sides facing, along the slanted and bottom edges. Edge-press seam allowances open. Turn right side out. Press. Repeat for remaining two C pieces. Position wrong sides of slanted pockets on top of B pieces. Pin in place. Sew in place along the bottom edges.

5. Sew two D pieces together along one 3¼" edge, right sides facing. Press seam allowance toward one side. Fold over along seam line, right sides out. Press. Repeat for remaining two D pieces. Position wrong sides of bottom pockets on B pieces, positioning the remaining 3¼" edge along the bottom edges.

6. Sew B pieces to B lining along one left and one right edge, right sides facing. Press seam allowance open. Fold over along seam line, right sides out. Press flat on seam.

7. Place A on work surface, right side up. Position wrong sides of full pockets on left- and right-side edges of overall pieces. Pin pocket in place.

8. Sew front/back of wallet to pocket inside of wallet, right sides facing, leaving a 2" opening along the bottom back edge.

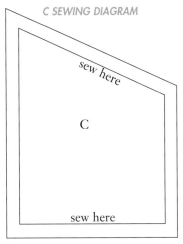

Enlarge pattern 200%.

41

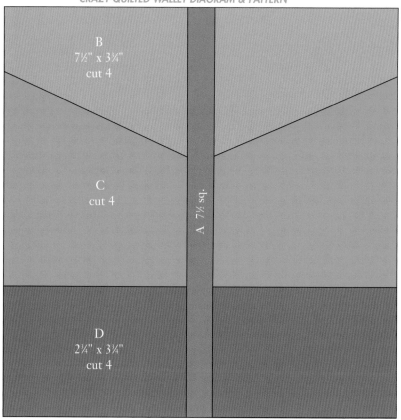

B
7½" x 3¾"
cut 4

C
cut 4

A 7½ sq.

D
2¾" x 3¾"
cut 4

Enlarge pattern 190%.

CRAZY-QUILTED WALLET DIAGRAM 2

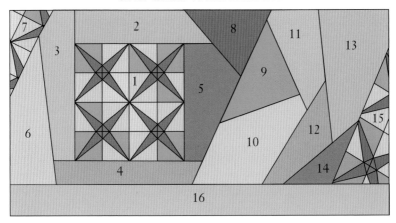

9. Edge-press seam allowance open. Clip bulk from corners.

Turn right side out through opening. Press flat.

10. Fold in half to close.

SILK APPLIQUÉ
HANDBAG

NEEDED ITEMS
- Fabrics
  - Muslin (10" x 12")
  - Silks (6½" x 10½" each) for outer side of handbag
    - Blue/green
    - Deep lime
    - Deep periwinkle
    - Golden tan
    - Pale seafoam (⅜ yd) for lining
    - Pale yellow
    - Periwinkle
    - Seafoam
- Circle templates (¾", 1⅛", 1¾")
- Fusible fleece (⅜ yd)
- Fusible interfacing, 22"-wide (1 yd)
- Magnetic closure, ¾"-wide
- Rope handbag handle with wooden triangle rings
- General Notions & Tools on page 7

SIZE
8½" bottom
7" top x 8½" tall

INSTRUCTIONS
*Note: Seam allowance ½"
unless otherwise indicated.*

PREPARATION
1. Refer to Silk Appliqué Handbag
Patterns on page 48. Using A for
front and back, trace two left and
two right-facing onto wrong side
of interfacing. Using B for front
and back, trace two left and two
right-facing pieces onto wrong

side of interfacing. Trace two D onto wrong side of interfacing. Cut each piece out close to traced lines.

2. Fuse two left A interfacing pieces onto wrong side of deep lime, and two right A interfacing pieces onto wrong side of deep periwinkle. Fuse two left B interfacing pieces onto wrong side of blue/green and two right B interfacing pieces onto wrong side of pale yellow. Fuse one D interfacing piece onto wrong side of periwinkle and one onto wrong side of golden tan. Cut pieces out along traced lines.

3. *Refer to photograph on page 45.* For front, sew one left and one right A pieces together where indicated on pattern, right sides facing. Sew one left and one right B pieces together where indicated on pattern, right sides facing. Press seam allowances open. Sew A unit to B unit where indicated on pattern, right sides facing, matching intersection. Press seam allowance open. Repeat Step 2 for back.

4. Using C, cut one each from muslin and fusible fleece. Trim away the ½" seam allowance from the fleece. Fuse fleece to wrong side of front.

5. Place tabs with right sides facing. Using ¼" seam allowance, sew along side and bottom edges. Clip seam allowance at curves to seam line. Edge press. Turn right side out. Position half of the magnetic closure on the golden tan side of the tab, about ½" up from bottom curved edge.

6. Cut two pieces 1½" x 2" from blue/green for handle loops. Press 1½" edges over ⅜" to wrong side of fabric. Set aside.

APPLIQUÉ
1. Trace E onto wrong side of seafoam. Trace F onto wrong side of periwinkle. Trace a portion of F onto wrong side of golden tan. Cut out each from fabric with ¼" seam allowance beyond traced lines.

2. *Refer to Freezer Paper Technique on pages 11–12.* Using freezer paper and circle template, cut out one of each circle.

3. Iron largest freezer paper circle onto wrong side of golden tan. Trim seam allowance to ¼".

SILK APPLIQUÉ HANDBAG DIAGRAM AND LINING PATTERN

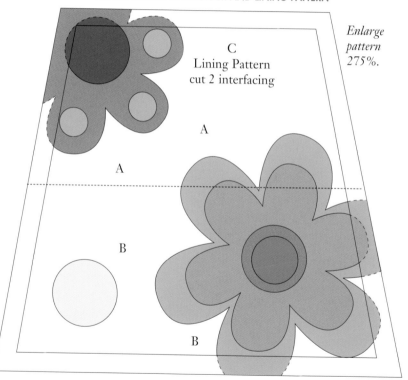

Enlarge pattern 275%.

C
Lining Pattern
cut 2 interfacing

A

A

B

B

4. Dab curved-edge seam allowance with spray starch. Clip seam allowance to curved paper edge.

5. Press curved fabric edges over edge of freezer paper. Remove freezer paper and press again. Repeat, using pale yellow and blue/green.

6. Prepare 1¼" circle for appliqué from deep lime. Prepare three ¾" circles from seafoam.

APPLIQUÉ FRONT
1. Place muslin on fleeced side of front. Safety-pin-baste layers together.

SILK APPLIQUÉ HANDBAG PATTERNS

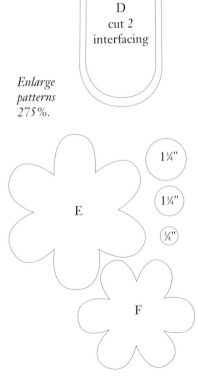

Enlarge patterns 275%.

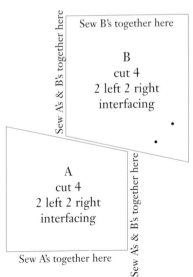

2. *Refer to Silk Appliqué Handbag Diagram on page 49.* Pin flowers to front where indicated on diagram. If desired, marginally baste-stitch appliqués in place.

3. *Refer to Needle-turn Technique on page 11.* Appliqué flowers onto front.

4. Appliqué prepared circles onto front where indicated on diagram. Hand-quilt front as desired.

HANDBAG

1. Sew front to back along side and bottom edges, right sides facing, matching intersections. Press seam allowances open.

2. Fold side edge to meet bottom edge, right sides facing, matching dots indicated on B. Stitch across corner. Repeat for remaining side and bottom edge.

3. Sew tab centered to upper edge of front. Slip handle loops through handle rings. Pin ends together. Pin and baste-stitch ends to upper edge of front at side seams.

FINISHING

1. Cut out two lining C pieces each from pale seafoam and fusible interfacing. Fuse interfacing to wrong side of each piece.

2. Sew lining in same manner as in steps 1–2 for Handbag, leaving a 4" opening along bottom edge. Do not turn right side out. Slip lining over handbag and align the top edges. Pin in place, matching side seams. Sew around top edge. Press seam allowance toward outer handbag.

3. Slip-stitch lining opening closed. Slip lining into bag. Press.

LOVED
HANGINGS

NEEDED ITEMS

- Cotton fabrics

    Blue/green marbled (¼ yd) for L and D letters,
        O and V bindings

    Hunter green leaf print (3½" x 4½" scrap) for E letter

    Muted olive (¼ yd) for L and E backgrounds

    Muted olive/cream stripe (¼ yd) for O and V
        backgrounds, L and E bindings

    Olive/light blue polka dots (¼ yd) for V letter,
        D binding

    Pale gold wavy striped (¼ yd) for D background

    Sage/blue green marbled (½ yd) for O letter, backing
        for all

- Cotton batting, 44"-wide (¼ yd)
- Silver ball chain (5')
- General Notions & Tools on page 7

SIZES

L–8½" x 11"

O–6¾" x 7½"

V–8½" x 11½"

E–5½" x 5¾"

D–8¾"x 10¼"

INSTRUCTIONS

PREPARATION

1. Enlarge and photocopy Loved
Hangings Patterns on page 53.
*Note: If you choose to use different
fonts from your computer, be certain
to use a different font for each letter,
varying the styles.* The letter L is

7¼" x 5½", letter O is 4" x 3¾", letter V is 8" x 5¼", letter E is 2¼" x 3½", letter D is 7" x 5¼". Make your lettering larger or smaller, as desired.

2. Trim around enlarged letters. Tape letters backward onto dull side of freezer paper. Cut out.

3. Cut background, backing, and batting pieces for each letter a bit larger than finished sizes will be. The backgrounds are 1½" wider on sides and top and 2" wider on bottom than each letter.

4. For L, cut pieces 9" x 11". For O, cut pieces 7¼" x 8". For V, cut pieces 9" x 12". For E, cut pieces 6" x 6¼". For D, cut pieces 9¼" x 11¼". Set aside backing and batting pieces.

APPLIQUÉ
1. *Refer to Freezer Paper Technique on pages 11–12.* Press shiny side of freezer paper onto wrong side of lettering fabrics. Trim seam allowance to ¼".

2. For each letter, dab curved-edge seam allowance with spray starch, clipping seam allowance at curved edges at inward points. Press fabric edges over edge of freezer paper. Remove freezer paper and press again. Repeat for each letter.

3. Pin prepared appliqué letters to background fabrics. Appliqué pieces in place. Press.

HAND QUILT
1. Layer backing, batting, and background fabrics. Baste-stitch layers together.

2. Using a doodling effect, hand-quilt around letters. If desired, quilt messages within each letter's background.

BINDING & FINISHING

1. Trim quilted letters. For L, trim to 8½" x 11". For O, trim to 6¾" x 7½". For V, trim to 8½" x 11½". For E, trim to 5" x 5¾". For D, trim to 8¼" x 10¼".

2. Cut 1¼" strips from binding fabrics to bind each quilted letter. Bind side edges, then top and bottom edges.

3. Cut five 12" lengths from the chain. Hand-stitch chain ends to top edges of quilted letters, spacing chain 4¼" apart along the top edge.

4. Hang and display letters at varying heights.

LOVED HANGINGS PATTERNS

Enlarge patterns 525%.

MOHAWK TRAIL
HANDBAG

NEEDED ITEMS
- Silk fabrics
    - Assorted scraps in browns and olives
        (12 variations 4" x 5" each) for piecework
    - Assorted scraps in golds, tans, and
        taupes (10 variations 4" x 5" each) for piecework
    - Gold dupioni (⅛ yd) for Back A, piecework
    - Light brown china (⅜ yd) for lining, inside pocket
    - Light gold matka (¼ yd) for Front A, B, C, Back B
    - Tan dupioni (¼ yd) for Back D, piecework
- Embroidery flosses: dark thistle, light thistle, medium
        mauve, olive green, pale gold
- Fusible fleece (⅜ yd)
- Fusible interfacing (¾ yd) for lining, inside pocket
- Rope/wood handbag handles (2)
- General Notions & Tools on page 7

SIZE
12" sq.

INSTRUCTIONS

PREPARATION
1. From light gold matka, cut four pieces 4" square for A front. Cut eight pieces 4" x 7" for B front and back. Cut one piece 7" square for C front. Cut two handle pieces 6" square.

2. Cut four gold dupioni pieces 4" square for A back. Cut one tan dupioni piece 7" square for C back.

3. From light brown china silk and fusible interfacing, cut two pieces from each 13" square for lining. Cut one piece from each, 13" x 9" for pocket. Cut two fusible fleece pieces 12" square.

APPLIQUÉ

1. Trace appliqué X and D backward onto dull side of freezer paper. Cut out. Repeat to make four of each pattern.

2. *Refer to Freezer Paper Technique on pages 11–12. Note: Appliqué edges are indicated on patterns with dots. Appliqué is on handbag front only.* Leave ¼" seam allowance along dotted edges, trimming remaining edges flush to paper. Dab seam allowance with spray starch. Press fabric edges up over designated edge of freezer paper. Remove paper and press again.

3. Use brown and olive scraps on B spaces. Prepare four appliqués from X and 20 appliqués from D for B spaces.

4. Use gold, tan, and taupe fabrics on A and C spaces. Prepare eight appliqués from X and 16 appliqués from D for A and C spaces.

5. *Refer to Mohawk Trail Handbag Assembly Diagram on page 59.* Pin prepared appliqué pieces to A, B, and C front pieces as indicated by the diagram. The outer edges of appliqué pieces are positioned ¼" inward from outer edges of the A, B, and C pieces. Appliqué pieces in place.

PIECE FRONT AND BACK

1. *Refer to Assembly Diagram on page 59.* Using ½" seam allowance, sew appliquéd front together in horizontal rows (A/B/A, B/C/B, etc.) Sew the horizontal rows together. Press seam allowances open. Sew back together in same manner.

EMBROIDER

1. *Refer to General Embroidery Stitches on pages 10–11.* Embroider a small area on the front, following Mohawk Trail Handbag Embroidery Diagram on page 57. Work pointed petals, combining light and dark thistle flosses, using the Bullion Lazy Daisy stitch.

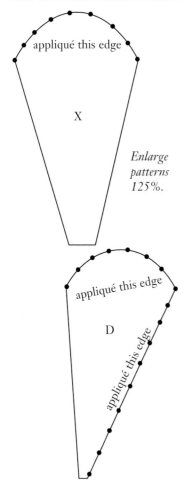

MOHAWK TRAIL HANDBAG PATTERNS

appliqué this edge

X

Enlarge patterns 125%.

appliqué this edge

D

appliqué this edge

appliqué this edge

MOHAWK TRAIL HANDBAG EMBROIDERY DIAGRAM

Stitch Key
- Lazy Daisy
- French Knot (thick)
- French Knot (light)
- Bullion
- Bullion Lazy Daisy

2. Work larger buds with medium mauve floss, using French knot.

3. Work smaller buds with light thistle floss, using French knot (use fewer strands.)

4. Work curved buds with pale gold floss, using bullion stitch.

5. Work tiny leaves with olive green floss, using lazy daisy stitch.

6. Fuse fleece onto wrong sides of front and back.

7. Sew front to back along side and bottom edges. Press seam allowance open.

8. To make corners, fold end from side seams to meet center of bottom, with right sides facing. Sew across corners ¾" inward from outer point. Press open.

HANDLES

1. Fold one handle piece in half. Sew across short ends. Trim corners. Turn right side out. Press. Repeat for remaining handle piece.

2. Slip handle piece through space on wooden handle. Align edges. Pin edges centered to top edge of front. Baste-stitch in place. Repeat for other handle piece and wooden handle.

LINING

1. Fuse interfacing onto wrong sides of lining and pocket pieces.

2. Press short ends of pocket piece under ½" to wrong side. Fold pocket in half, right sides facing, aligning pressed-under edges. Sew sides. Trim corners. Turn right side out. Press.

3. Position pocket centered on lining back. Sew to back along side and bottom edges. Sew lining front to back along side and bottom edges, leaving a 5" opening along one side edge. Press seam allowance open.

4. To make corners, fold end from side seams to meet center of bottom, with right sides facing. Sew across corners ¾" inward from outer point. Press open.

FINISHING

1. Slip lining over handbag, right sides facing. Sew around top

edges. Press seam allowance toward lining. Turn right side out and slip lining into bag. Press along top edge.

2. Slip-stitch opening closed. Hand- or machine-topstitch around top edge.

MOHAWK TRAIL HANDBAG ASSEMBLY DIAGRAM

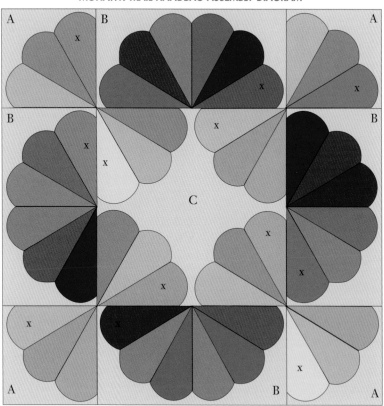

Wool Appliqué
Pillow

NEEDED ITEMS
- Washable wool fabrics, 44"-wide
    - Black (⅛ yd) for front
    - Ecru (¼ yd) for front/back
    - Gold (¼ yd) for front/back
- Wool felt, assorted colors
    - 1" sq. (16)
    - 2" sq. (16)
    - 3" sq. (16)
- Black buttons (2), any size
- Black thread
- Pillow form (16")
- General Notions & Tools on page 7

SIZE
16" sq.

INSTRUCTIONS

PREPARATION
1. From black wool, cut two pieces 4½" x 16½" for striped front. From ecru wool, cut one piece 4½" x 16½" for striped front and one piece 8½" x 16½" for back.

From gold wool, cut one piece 4½" x 16½" for striped front and one piece 8½" x 16½" for back.

2. Sew 4½" x 16½" pieces for striped front together, right sides facing, using a ¼" seam allowance, forming striped front backdrop for appliquéd squares. Press seam allowances open.

3. For appliqué squares, use as many shades of wool or felt scraps as possible, with the goal of achieving a granny-square afghan effect.

4. Layer squares onto striped backdrop. When pleased with color arrangement, pin squares together and to the backdrop.

APPLIQUÉ

1. Using doubled black thread, whipstitch 1" and 2" squares to 3" squares. Press layered squares.

2. Hand-stitch layered squares to striped backdrop in same manner as Step 1.

SEW FRONT TO BACK

1. Cut two slits along one edge of gold piece for back, spacing slits at one-third intervals along edge. Make slits ⅛" longer than diameter of button. Whipstitch around slits, if desired.

2. Overlap back edge with slits onto ecru piece for back. Pin appliquéd front to overlapping backs, wrong sides facing, aligning all edges. Using a ¼" seam allowance, hand- or machine-sew front and back together.

FINISHING

1. Stitch buttons in place.

2. Slip pillow form into pillow. Button closed.

CLAMSHELL APPLIQUÉ
PILLOW

NEEDED ITEMS

- Silk fabrics
    - Bright pink/fuchsia (5 variations 3" x 6" each)
        for clamshells
    - Coral/light orange (3 variations 3" x 6" each)
        for clamshells
    - Light pink (3 variations 3" x 6" each) for clamshells
    - Red/orange (6 variations 3" x 6" each) for clamshells
    - Taupe (½ yd) for pillow front, back
    - Yellow-orange (¼ yd) for clamshells, pillow border
- Ribbons
    - Bright pink satin, 1½"-wide (1⅛ yd)
    - Silk (5" each) for rosettes
        - dark rose, 4mm
        - fuchsia, 4mm
        - orange, 4mm
- Embroidery floss, light mauve
- Lightweight fusible interfacing, 22"-wide (1 yd)
- Pillow form (16")
- General Notions & Tools on page 7

INSTRUCTIONS

PREPARATION

1. From taupe silk fabric and fusible interfacing, cut one piece each 15½"-square for pillow front. Cut two pieces each 15½" x 9½"for pillow back.

2. Cut one 5½" x 36" from yellow-orange fabric. Fuse interfacing onto back side of piece. Cut eight strips 1¼" x 18" from interfaced piece.

3. Using Clamshell Pattern, cut six clams from freezer paper.

4. Refer to Clamshell Appliqué Diagram on page 66. *Notes: Each shade of silk fabric for the clamshell appliqué is used to make approximately two clamshells, for a total of 39 clamshells.*

   All upper curved edges are prepared for appliqué. The left- and right-side curved edges are prepared for appliqué if clamshell is along outer-left or outer-right side.

All edges are prepared for appliqué for the bottom-tip clamshell.

5. *Refer to Freezer Paper Technique on pages 11–12.* For each clamshell, iron freezer-paper template onto wrong side of silk fabric. Dab seam allowance along designated edge with spray starch. Press fabric edges over edge of template. Remove and press again. Reuse templates.

CLAMSHELL PATTERN

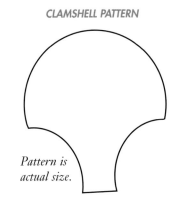

Pattern is actual size.

6. Using disappearing-ink pen, lightly mark pillow front vertically through center only. *Note: Do not draw line from edge to edge. This line will be used to keep the middle column of clamshells centered.*

7. Lightly mark a horizontal line across pillow front 4½" down from upper edge and through the center of the front. *Note: Do not draw lines from edge to edge. This will be used for placement of the curved top edge of the second row of clamshells.*

8. Beginning with second row, pin clamshells to pillow front along drawn horizontal line, utilizing center vertical line.

9. Pin first row in place, slipping bottom edges from first row of clamshells underneath top edge of second row of clamshells.

10. Continue placing clamshells with each row ⅝" below the previous, and making certain the outer edge clamshells have an

appropriate finished edge to appliqué. Baste-stitch clamshells in place.

APPLIQUÉ
1. Hand-stitch each clamshell in place. Press when completed.

MAKE PILLOW
1. If necessary, trim pillow front so it remains square. Hem long edge of each pillow back with a doubled ¾" hem.

2. Cut satin ribbon into two equal lengths. Sew each length to the vertical center of each hemmed back.

3. Overlap backs so they are identical in size to the front.

4. Using ¼" seam allowance, sew one yellow/orange interfaced strip to each pillow front outer edge, right sides facing, and extending strip beyond both corners along each edge. Press seam allowance toward strip.

5. Miter strips at each corner. Press seam allowances open.

6. Repeat Steps 1–5 for back.

7. Using ½" seam allowance, sew front to back, right sides facing. Trim bulk from corners. Press seam allowances open as much as possible. Turn pillow right side out.

FINISHING

1. Make three tiny rosettes from 4mm silk ribbon.

2. Embroider Bullion Lazy Daisy leaves on three clamshells.

3. Hand-stitch rosettes in place near leaves.

4. Slip pillow form into pillow, tie closed with ribbon.

Sailboat Appliqué
Pillow

NEEDED ITEMS

- Cotton fabrics for ocean/sky designs
    - Blue sky (⅛ yd) for spaces 2, 3, 5
        - (use wrong side for space 5)
    - Bright blue sky (⅛ yd) for space 6
    - Bright turquoise/silver metallic variegated (⅛ yd)
        - for spaces 7, 18
    - Light turquoise sky (⅛ yd) for spaces 1, 8
        - (use wrong side for space 1)
    - Lime green variegated (3" x 4") for 20, 21, 22
    - Seafoam variegated (⅛ yd) for spaces 4, 15
    - Stormy ocean (⅛ yd) for spaces 14, 17
    - Stormy sky (⅛ yd) for spaces 13, 19
    - Vibrant turquoise variegated (⅛ yd) for spaces 9, 16
    - White broadcloth (½ yd)
        - for spaces 10, 11, 12, front foundation
    - White textured (⅓ yd) for pillow back
- Clear glass buttons, 1" (2)
- Embroidery floss, taupe-brown
- Pillow form (16")
- General Notions & Tools on page 7

69

SIZE
16" sq.

INSTRUCTIONS

PREPARATION

1. Enlarge and photocopy Sailboat Appliqué Pillow Pattern on page 72.

2. Using pencil, trace design onto 18"-square piece of white broadcloth.

3. Make a pattern for space 1 by tracing space onto a piece of paper. Add ¼" seam allowance along top and bottom edges. Add ½" seam allowance at side edges. Cut out pattern.

4. Working with light turquoise sky fabric, cut one from wrong side of fabric. Pin piece 1 in place on white broadcloth front backing.

5. Place enlarged design wrong side up.

6. Tape two pieces of quilter's freezer paper together along shorter edges.

7. Beginning with spaces 2 and 3, trace space onto dull side of freezer paper. Mark bottom edge of both pieces with an "x." Cut out.

8. Trace remaining pieces sky, ocean, and boat pieces onto dull side of freezer paper. For all remaining sky and ocean spaces, mark an "x" along the top edges of each piece. Cut out each piece.

APPLIQUÉ

1. *Refer to Freezer Paper Technique on pages 11–12.* Iron freezer paper template piece onto wrong side of fabrics for that space as indicated in the Needed Items list. *Note: For spaces 1 and 5, the wrong side of the fabric has been used as the right side.* Dab seam allowance along edge marked with an "x" with spray starch. Press fabric edges over edge of template. Remove and press.

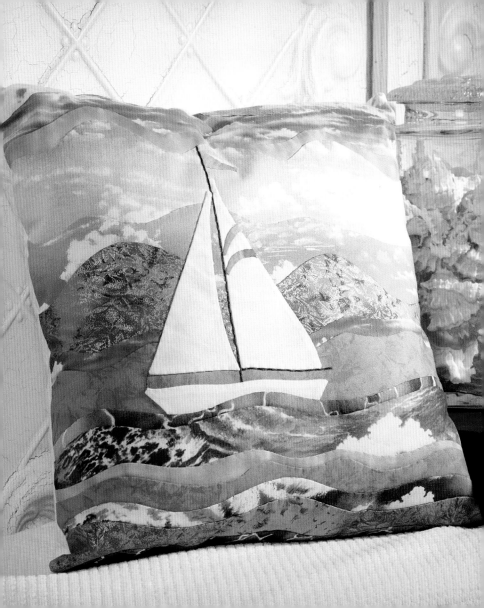

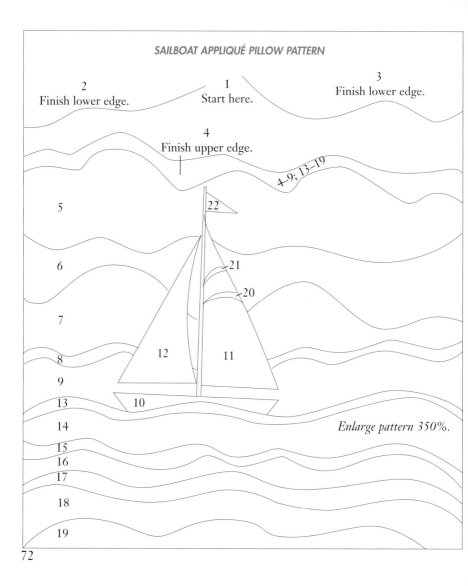

SAILBOAT APPLIQUÉ PILLOW PATTERN

2
Finish lower edge.

1
Start here.

3
Finish lower edge.

4
Finish upper edge.

4–9; 13–19

5

6

7

8

9

13

14

15

16

17

18

19

22

21

20

12

11

10

Enlarge pattern 350%.

2. Position each prepared piece in place in numerical order on the front backing. Baste-stitch in place.

3. Hand-stitch pieces in place. Press stitching occasionally during the hand-stitching process and press when completed.

4. Using one strand of floss, couch-stitch six strands for sailboat mast and boom.

5. Trim front to 17" square.

MAKE PILLOW

1. Cut two pieces 17" x 10½" from white textured fabric for pillow back.

2. Hem one long edge of each pillow back with doubled ¾" hem.

3. Make two 1⅛"-long buttonholes along hemmed edge of one back.

4. Overlap backs onto front, right sides facing, placing hemmed back with buttonholes down first.

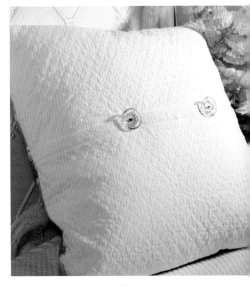

5. Using a ½" seam allowance, sew front to back. Trim bulk from corners. Press seam allowances open as much as possible. Turn right side out.

6. Stitch buttons in place on the remaining hemmed back.

FINISH

1. Slip pillow form into pillow. Button closed.

DRESDEN PLATE WITH HEXAGONS PILLOW

NEEDED ITEMS
- Cotton flannel fabrics, variegated
  Green-yellow (⅛ yd) for B
  Pink-coral-yellow (½ yd) for A
- Polyester stuffing (12 oz)
- Posterboard
- General Notions & Tools on page 7

SIZE
15" dia.

INSTRUCTIONS

PREPARATION
1. Using A on page 77, cut 24 pieces (12 for front, 12 for back) from pink-coral-yellow flannel fabric. Use variegated shades in the fabric as desired. Mark cut pieces with dots on fabric wrong side as indicated on pattern.

PIECE PILLOW FRONT AND BACK
1. Using a ¼" seam allowance, hand- or machine-sew twelve A pieces together for pillow front along long edges, right sides facing. Begin and end stitching at dots. Press seam allowances open. Repeat for remaining twelve A sections for pillow back.

2. Using C, cut one from posterboard. *Note: When freezer paper is removed from flannel fabric, an excess of fuzz remains on freezer paper, causing it to not be reusable. If fabric of choice is not flannel freezer paper pieces can be used.*

3. Place posterboard piece on wrong side of one front section, placing posterboard curved edge ½" down from fabric curved edge. Dab curved seam allowance with spray starch. Press fabric curved edge over cardboard curved edge.

74

Remove cardboard and press again. Repeat for each front and back section. Press again.

1. *Refer to Freezer Paper Technique on pages 11–12.* Using B, cut eight pieces from freezer paper, seven for front and one for pillow back.

2. Press freezer paper hexagons onto wrong side of green-yellow flannel. Use variegated shades in fabric as desired. Trim, leaving ¼" seam allowance around each. Dab seam allowance with spray starch. Press fabric edges over designated edge of freezer paper. *Note: Hexagon freezer-paper pieces are not removed until hexagon fabric pieces have been sewn together.*

3. Place two hexagons together with right sides facing. Hand-stitch along one edge. Fold open.

4. Continue hand-stitching hexagons together in this manner to form pillow front center. Remove freezer paper. Press.

5. Position stitched hexagon piece centered onto pillow front. Hand-stitch in place.

6. Position remaining hexagon piece centered onto pillow back. Hand-stitch in place.

1. Using whipstitch, stitch front to back along outer curved edges, leaving two sections not sewn.

2. Stuff pillow with polyfil through opening. Continue to stitch remaining sections together, stuffing a bit while stitching, until pillow is completely stuffed and stitched closed.

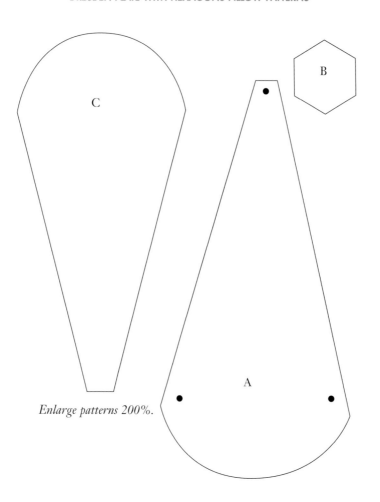

Enlarge patterns 200%.

Violet Stencil
PILLOW

NEEDED ITEMS

- Fabrics
  Copper brown silk dupioni (¼ yd) for stencil design
  Plum/brown silk brocade (1 yd)
      for pillow front and back
- Beads
  Copper seed 11/0 (12)
  Copper variegated triangle cut seed 11/0 (6)
  Olive green flat round 6mm (12)
- Cotton batting, 44"-wide (15" x 22")
- Embroidery floss
  Burgundy
  Copper metallic
- Embroidery needles
    size 18–20 chenille
    size 5
- Pillow form, 14" x 21"
- Silk ribbon, brown 4mm (1 yd) for pillow back closure
- General Notions & Tools on page 7

SIZE
14" x 21"

INSTRUCTIONS
PREPARATION
1. Cut brocade for pillow front and back 22" wide x 35" (front and back are all one piece.)

2. Press 22" edges under ¼" to fabric wrong side. Press under again. Using machine, hem close to pressed-under edge. Machine-overcast 35" edges.

3. For determining design placement, mark pillow front

with pins, placing pins 19" from lower hemmed edge.

PILLOW FRONT DESIGN
1. Enlarge and photocopy Violet Stencil Pillow Pattern.

2. Trace each design element onto matte side of freezer paper.

APPLIQUÉ
1. *Refer to Freezer Paper Technique on pages 11–12.* Iron freezer paper pieces onto wrong side of copper brown dupioni, allowing for necessary seam allowances.

2. Clip fabric at inward points and curves. Dab seam allowance along edges with spray starch. Press fabric edges over edge of freezer paper. Remove paper. Press.

3. Using 19" pin-marked line as a bottom edge guide for design, position each piece on pillow front. *Note: Working with silk dupioni and the intricate pieces for this design are tricky, especially at the inward points and curves. Don't worry about imperfections in the pressing process, as the couched floss will cover-up any problem areas.*

VIOLET STENCIL PILLOW PATTERN

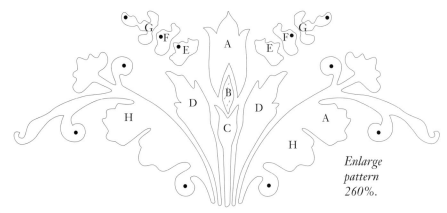

Enlarge pattern 260%.

4. Baste, then hand-stitch pieces in place. Press occasionally during hand-stitching process and press when completed.

EMBROIDER AND BEAD

1. Layer pillow front with batting. Baste in place.

2. Position six strands of metallic floss along outer edge of one design element. Using one strand of burgundy, couch-stitch around metallic floss design element to create an outlined effect. Using size 18–20 chenille needle, bring metallic floss to surface, knotting floss on underside. Use size 5 needle for couching strand. Repeat for each element.

3. Invisibly overlap metallic floss at beginning/ending once a design element has been outlined.

4. Hand-stitch 6mm beads onto appliquéd and embroidered design where indicated on pattern, using copper seed beads to anchor each.

5. Hand-stitch triangle-cut seed beads in place onto B.

MAKE PILLOW

1. Overlap top hemmed edge 5" over bottom hemmed edge, aligning the side edges. Turn wrong side out.

2. Using ½" seam allowance, sew side edges, right sides facing. Press seam allowances open. Turn pillow right side out.

3. Make 14" x 21" pillow form from muslin fabric. Insert form into pillow back.

FINISHING

1. Cut 4mm ribbon into two lengths. Sew ribbon pieces to back overlap through both layers. Tie ribbons into knotted bows to help keep back closed.

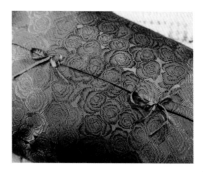

OVERSIZED ROSE CANVAS

NEEDED ITEMS

- Cotton fabrics
    - Bright pink variegated (¼ yd) for 1, 14
    - Bright rose iridescent brocade (¼ yd) for 2, 4
    - Gold brocade (⅛ yd) for 22, 23
    - Pink brocade (¼ yd) for 11, 13
    - Pink/yellow variegated (¼ yd) for 6, 7, 16, 19
- Metallic scrap
    - Bright pink (torn strip that is ¾" x 11")
- Silk fabrics
    - Celedon dupioni (⅛ yd) for 24
    - Drab olive dupioni (⅛ yd) for 25
    - Orange dupioni (⅛ yd) for 3, 10
    - Pale yellow dupioni (⅛ yd) for 17, 21
    - Petal pink dupioni (¼ yd) for 12, 18
    - Pink dupioni (⅛ yd) for 8, 20
- Wool fabrics
    - Cream felt (1 yd) for background
    - Rose (¼ yd) for 5, 9, 15
- Visual edge stretched canvas (20" sq.)
- Gold iridescent heart-shaped beads, 5mm (18)
- Staple gun
- General Notions & Tools on page 7

SIZE
20" sq.

INSTRUCTIONS

PREPARATION

1. Enlarge and photocopy pillow front design. *Note: Most elements*

overlap onto each other, except for 23; all edges are finished for this piece.

2. Using pencil, trace portions of the design centered onto cream felt. *Note: It is not necessary to trace entire design, just enough to help with placement of pieces.* Place enlarged design wrong side up.

1. The design is created in numerical order with 2 overlapping 1, 5 overlapping onto 3 and 4 etc. Create a freezer paper piece for each element. Beginning with piece 1, trace design element onto dull side of freezer paper. Mark edges that will be finished for appliqué. Determine the edges that will be an underlap for the adjacent pieces. Add ½" to the freezer paper pattern along the underlapping edges. Cut out.

2. *Refer to Freezer Paper Technique on pages 11–12.* Iron freezer-paper piece onto wrong side of fabric for 1. Dab seam allowance along finished edges with spray starch. Press fabric edges over edge of freezer paper. Remove freezer paper and press again.

3. Position and pin prepared petal 1 in place on background fabric.

4. Continue to prepare petal and leaf pieces, pinning them in place as you go. Baste-stitch in place.

5. Continue to prepare petals and leaf pieces, pinning them in place as you go. Reposition pieces if necessary. Baste-stitch pieces in place. *Note: As each piece is added to the background, it will become more clear as to which edges should be finished for appliqué.*

6. Hand-stitch petals and leaf in place. Press occasionally during hand-stitching process. Press when completed.

7. Gather-stitch down center of ¼"-wide torn metallic fabric strip. Pull gathers tightly. Hand-stitch gathered strip around curved edges of rose center.
9. Hand-stitch beads in place amidst gathered metallic strip.

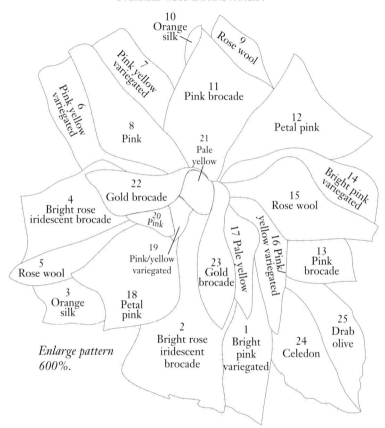

10
Orange
silk

9
Rose wool

7
Pink-yellow
variegated

11
Pink brocade

6
Pink-yellow
variegated

12
Petal pink

8
Pink

21
Pale
yellow

14
Bright pink
variegated

22
Gold brocade

15
Rose wool

4
Bright rose
iridescent brocade

20
Pink

17 Pale yellow

16 Pink/yellow variegated

19
Pink/yellow
variegated

23
Gold
brocade

13
Pink
brocade

5
Rose wool

3
Orange
silk

18
Petal
pink

2
Bright rose
iridescent
brocade

1
Bright
pink
variegated

25
Drab
olive

24
Celedon

*Enlarge pattern
600%.*

FINISHING

1. Center finished appliqué over canvas. Snugly wrap background fabric around canvas and staple edges to inner back-side edge of canvas. Trim bulk from corners. *Note: Some outer petal corners will wrap onto the side edges of the canvas.*

85

CHILDREN WALL HANGING

CHILDREN
WALL HANGING

Project 16

NEEDED ITEMS

- Fabrics

    Ivory cotton, textured (7" x 29½") for B background

    Mustard yellow linen (½ yd) for A, C, backing

    Orange linen (2" wide strip x width of goods) for side binding, hanging loops

    Variegated cottons, 7 different assorted light shades (4½" x 5½" each) for bodies

    Wool felt scraps for clothing, hair, hat

        Aqua, light blue, light green, lime green, medium blue, peach, periwinkle, rust, teal

- Cotton batting (9" x 29")
- General Notions & Tools on page 7

SIZE

9" x 28½"

INSTRUCTIONS

PREPARATION

1. From mustard yellow linen, cut one piece 10½" x 29½" for upper strip A/backing piece and one piece 5" x 29½".

2. Cut from orange linen two strips 2" x 10" and three strips 2" x 5½".

3. Trace portions of children's bodies to the piece of ivory textured cotton. *Note: It is not necessary to trace entire design, just enough to help with body placement.*

4. Cut out two bodies from freezer paper.

5. Make a posterboard pattern for each basic item of clothing: dress with long sleeves, pants,

shirt with long sleeves. *Note: If desired, make a posterboard pattern for different hairdos and the hat. The patterns will make clothing and hairdo tracing easier.*

APPLIQUÉ BODIES

1. *Refer to Freezer Paper Technique on pages 11–12.* Iron freezer paper piece onto wrong side of fabric for one body. Clip all inward curves and points. Dab seam allowance with spray starch. Press fabric edges over edge of freezer paper. Remove freezer paper and press again. Repeat for each body. Reuse freezer-paper bodies.

2. Position and pin bodies onto background fabric. Hand-stitch bodies in place. Press.

APPLIQUÉ CLOTHING

Note: The children can be dressed with a variety of different shades of wool felt. An easy way to accomplish this is to cut out the basic clothing items, then add to the basics by using dress and shirt designs.

1. Cut one dress each from lime, medium blue peach, and teal felt.

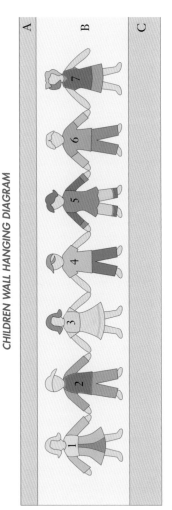

CHILDREN WALL HANGING DIAGRAM

2. Cut one pants each from aqua, lime, periwinkle, and rust felt scraps.

3. Cut one shirt each from aqua, light green, and medium blue felt scraps.

4. Cut accents for dresses and shirts from felt scraps as desired.

5. Cut hairdos, hat and hair bow from felt scraps. Pin accents to dresses, shirts or pants and hand-stitch in place.

6. Pin clothing, hair bow, hairdos, and hat onto bodies and hand-stitch in place. Press well.

FINISHING

1. Layer cotton batting underneath appliquéd section, placing section ½" down from one edge of batting.

2. Using ½" seam allowance, sew one long edge of 10½" x 29½" piece of mustard yellow linen to upper edge of appliquéd section/batting. Press piece upward. Fold piece over top edge of batting to back side of batting, forming top border A and backing for the wall hanging. Stitch wall hanging front to backing by stitching in the ditch just below seam line for border A. Trim excess backing flush with batting along bottom edge.

3. Sew one long edge of 5" x 29½" piece of mustard yellow linen to lower appliquéd section, through batting and backing. Press piece downward. Fold piece over bottom edge of batting to back side, forming bottom border C. Turn remaining long edge under ½" and pin in place along strip seam line. Hand-stitch in place. Trim side edges. Bind side edges with 10"-long orange linen strips.

4. Working with 5½"-long orange linen strips, press long edges to center. Press in half. Stitch along both edges. Repeat for each strip. Form loops with strips. Hand-stitch loops to back of wall hanging along upper edge.

CHILDREN WALL HANGING PATTERNS

#7

Enlarge patterns 165%.

Body

#4

#7

#1, 3

#6

#5

#2

#3

#6

#4

#1

#7

#2

#5

#5

#2, 4, 6

91

BUTTERFLY CHRISTMAS
STOCKING

NEEDED ITEMS
- Fabrics
    Sherpa-backed faux suede, mint green (⅓ yd) for
       stocking front and back
    Washable wool, ivory (5" x 5") for butterfly wings
- Pearls by the yard, 4mm (2") for butterfly body
- Seed beads, mint green 11/0
- General Notions & Tools on page 7

SIZE
18" x 8"

INSTRUCTIONS

PREPARATION
1. Cut one stocking front and back and one 6" x ½" strip from faux suede.

2. Machine-overcast outer edges of stocking front, back, and narrow strip.

3. Cut one A and B from posterboard.

4. Cut two A and B from washable wool ⅛" larger all around than patterns.

APPLIQUÉ
1. Place posterboard onto A fabric, wrong side up. Steam-press curved fabric edges over edge of posterboard. Remove posterboard and press again. Repeat for remaining wing A fabric. Repeat this step for B fabric and posterboard.

2. Position wings (A and B) on stocking front and hand-stitch in place.

3. Hand-stitch pearl strand in place for butterfly body.

4. Hand-stitch seed beads onto stocking front, following curved design line.

MAKE STOCKING
1. Pin stocking front to back, sherpa sides facing. Using ¼" seam allowance, sew together along side and bottom edges.

2. Fold top edge down about 3" to form stocking cuff.

FINISHING
1. Fold narrow strip in half to form loop. Hand-stitch loop ends to inside top-left edge of stocking, below cuff fold line.

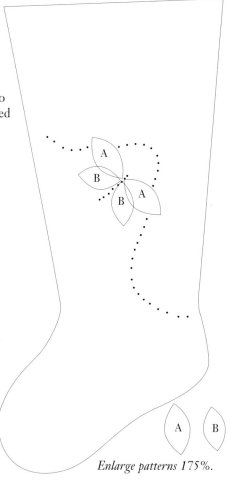

Enlarge patterns 175%.

ABOUT THE AUTHOR

Mary Jo Hiney has been an author with Sterling/Chapelle since 1992. As a freelance designer, Mary Jo also contributes her design skills to other enterprises in the fabric and craft industries, including her own line of packaged silks and patterns.

Mary Jo has a love for fabric and sewing that she credits to her mom, when, as a child, together they would visit the local fabric store and savor the loveliness in each bolt of fabric and the excitement for the project in mind. Her mother began teaching Mary Jo to embroider at age three, allowing her to redo time and again her youthful stitches. Mary Jo was taught the art of quilting by her sister, Rose, who continues to inspire her.

Mary Jo lives with her husband and children on the treasured Central Coast of California.

METRIC CONVERSION CHART

Inches	cm	Inches	cm	Inches	cm	Inches	cm
⅛	0.3	1¼	3.2	4	10.2	10	25.4
¼	0.6	1½	3.8	4½	11.4	11	27.9
½	1.3	1¾	4.4	5	12.7	12	30.5
⅝	1.6	2	5.1	6	15.2	13	33.0
¾	1.9	2½	6.4	7	17.8	14	35.6
⅞	2.2	3	7.6	8	20.3	15	38.1
1	2.5	3½	8.9	9	22.9	16	40.6

INDEX

Applying a Zipper 8

Backstitch 10

Basting 8

Batting 8

Beading 8

Binding 9

Bullion 10

Bullion Lazy Daisy 10

Butterfly Christmas
    Stocking 92–94

Children Wall Hanging . . . 86–91

Clamshell Appliqué Pillow . 63–68

Couching 10

Crazy-quilted Wallet 38–43

Designer Shoe Travel
    Pouch 28–32

Dresden Plate with Hexagons
    Pillow 74–77

Dutch Windmill
    Stocking 33–37

Edge-pressing 9

Elephant Appliqué Cosmetic
    Case 18–22

Embroidery Stitches 10–11

Freezer Paper Technique . . 11–12

French Knot 10

General Notions & Tools 7

Introduction 6

Lazy Daisy 11

Loved Hangings 50–53

Making Yo-yos 12

Metric Conversion Chart 95

Mohawk Trail Handbag . . . 54–59

Needle-turn Technique 13

Oversized Rose Canvas 82–85

Pressing 9

Quilting Basics 7–13

Robbing Peter to Pay Paul
    Coin Purse 23–27

Sailboat Appliqué Pillow . . 69–73

Silk Appliqué Handbag 44–49

Transferring an Appliqué Design
    onto Fabric 13

Violet Stencil Pillow 78–81

Whipstitch 11

Wool Appliqué Pillow 60–62

Working with Patterns 13

Yo-yo Eyeglass Case 14–17